the little book of
DREAMS

Published by OH!
20 Mortimer Street
London W1T 3JW

Disclaimer:
This book and the information contained herein are for general
educational and entertainment use only. The contents are not claimed to
be exhaustive, and the book is sold on the understanding that neither the
publishers nor the author are thereby engaged in rendering any kind of
professional services. Users are encouraged to confirm the information
contained herein with other sources and review the information
carefully with their appropriate, qualified service providers. Neither the
publishers nor the author shall have any responsibility to any person
or entity regarding any loss or damage whatsoever, direct or indirect,
consequential, special or exemplary, caused or alleged to be caused, by
the use or misuse of information contained in this book.

ISBN 978-1-80069-167-4

Editorial: Victoria Godden
Project manager: Russell Porter
Design: Luke Griffin
Production: Freencky Portas

A CIP catalogue record for this book is available from the British Library

Printed in China

10 9 8 7 6 5 4 3 2 1

the little book of
DREAMS

lisa dyer

CONTENTS

"The interpretation of dreams is a great art."

PARACELSUS

INTRODUCTION

Navigate the uncharted territory of your dreams to reveal your innermost thoughts, feelings and motivations. Whether you dream of flying or falling, being late or lost, you will find interpretations to the most common dreams on the following pages.

Analyzing your dreams is a very individual act – you alone created the images you see and the emotions you feel! Some dreams will be obvious hangovers from your day, re-enactments of events or issues on your mind; dreaming about public speaking or a date, for example, can mean you are subconsciously rehearsing for a waking-life event.

6

Notice these direct references and "day residue", but look deeper. Your dream landscape is rich with potent symbolism and imagery, so take note of its inhabitants, locations and events. The interpretations on the following pages will help you identify the symbols and archetypes that appear in your dreams, which can guide you on a journey of self-discovery.

A fantastic self-help tool, dreams provide direct feedback to the dreamer – they can tell you about your relationships, desires and fears. Interpreting the emotional and visual language of dreams helps you work through your experiences and find answers to problems weighing on your mind. Most of all, dreams are the gateway to a happier, fulfilled and more self-aware life.

CHAPTER

1

DREAM
SLEEP

Discover dream folklore and fact, and reveal the significance of your dreams by understanding and maximizing your dream sleep.

"A dream which is not interpreted is like a letter which is not read."

THE TALMUD

The word dream originates from the Middle English *dreme*, meaning to rejoice, sing and make music.

The Hawaiian word for dream, *moe'uhane*, translates as "soul sleep" and is considered a way to communicate with the gods and ancestor spirits, who offer guidance, prophecy, inspiration and the healing of relationships and the body.

In Greek mythology, Morpheus, the son of Hypnos, the god of sleep, had the ability to enter the dreams of mortal men and deliver messages from the gods. He first appeared in Ovid's *Metamorphoses*.

The Egyptian Dream Book, a papyrus found in Deir el-Medina, near the Valley of Kings, and dating from the reign of Ramesses II (1279–1213 BCE), is the oldest dream interpretation guide, recording 108 positive and negative dreams.

In Japan, it is believed that if you can't sleep at night, it is because you are awake in someone else's dream. The Japanese also believe that the first dream you have in the new year, known as *hatsuyume*, foretells your luck for the coming year.

Baku is the Japanese dream-eater, a protective spirit often taking the form of a chimera with the legs of a tiger and the head of an elephant, who visits homes in the middle of the night to devour nightmares.

The Ojibwe Native American tribe believes dreamcatchers represent Asibikaashi, the Spider Woman, who weaves protective charms for those sleeping. Like Asibikaashi, the dreamcatcher will trap bad dreams in its web while the hole in the centre lets good dreams through.

In the Native American Abenaki tribe, dreaming is associated with the creation story: the Great Spirit created all the inhabitants of the earth in a dream while asleep on the Great Turtle's back.

To induce vivid dreams, the indigenous
Chontal of the Mexican state of Oaxaca
use the flowering shrub *Calea zacatechichi*,
while the seeds of *Entada rheedii* are
similarly used in various African cultures.

Clary sage, valerian, mugwort and
ashwagandha are just a few of the many
herbs and plants thought to aid in dream
sleep. *Salvia divinorum* has been used
for thousands of years for oneiromancy
(dream divination).

"The interpretation of dreams is the royal road to a knowledge of the unconscious activities of the mind."

SIGMUND FREUD

The Interpretation of Dreams (1899)

According to Freud, dreams have manifest and latent content. The manifest is often surreal and nonsensical, while the latent content is the real meaning of the dream.

He developed a free association technique, where you begin with one dream symbol and then follow with what first springs to mind. Continue in this way to see where your interpretation leads.

Freud thought dreams represented unconscious desires, motivations and wish fulfilment. Although some of his ideas have been debunked, scientific studies show that repressed thoughts and emotions do emerge in dreams in what is known as "dream rebound".

"*Dreams are never concerned with trivia.*"

SIGMUND FREUD

The Interpretation of Dreams (1899)

We may dream to forget. One theory suggests that dreams serve to clean up the clutter of our waking experiences, clearing information that we don't need and retaining what is important, like a computer memory reboot.

Researchers such as psychiatrist Allan Hobson promote the idea of protoconsciousness – that dreaming involves constructing a virtual reality in our minds that we can use as a self-help tool to resolve issues during our waking life.

Image rehearsal therapy (IRT) can help rewrite a nightmare. Write down the nightmare and then reframe the content, and the outcome, from negative to positive. Mentally rehearse the new positive story. If it's a recurring nightmare, rehearse the new story every day.

Practitioners of dream therapy and cognitive behavioural therapy (CBT) focus on the dreamer rather than the dream, and the communication between the unconscious and conscious mind in the individual.

the
FOUR STAGES
of SLEEP

Understanding the different stages
of sleep can help you maximize
your dream sleep and recall.

1. This transition to sleep stage lasts five to ten minutes and is characterized by non-rapid eye movements (NREM), muscle relaxation, lower body temperature and a slower heart rate.

2. Light sleep accounts for 50 per cent of your sleep time and occurs for up to 20 minutes for each cycle. Eye movements stop, you are less aware of your surroundings and your breathing and heartbeat become more regular.

3. Deep or delta sleep is essential for physical repairs and memory retention. Noises or activity may fail to wake you.

4. Rapid eye movement (REM) or dream sleep occurs at about 90 minutes after the onset of sleep. Blood pressure rises, the heart rate speeds up, respiration becomes erratic and brain activity increases. Involuntary muscles also become immobilized to prevent you from acting out your dreams. Most of dreaming occurs in this stage. If you wake up here, you are more likely to remember your dreams.

"REM-sleep dreaming has been shown to take the painful sting out of difficult, even traumatic, emotional episodes experienced during the day, offering emotional resolution when you awake the next morning."

MATTHEW WALKER

author of *Why We Sleep* (2017)

Sleep stages repeat themselves throughout the night. As the cycle repeats, you will spend less time in stages 1 to 3 and more time dreaming in stage 4. Although dreams can occur in any of the four stages, the most vivid and memorable dreams occur in REM.

"There is no denial in
the dream time, only
subconscious and
spiritual truths."

PAMELA CUMMINS
Learn the Secret Language of Dreams (2016)

"When your eyes are darting around during REM sleep, they are scanning the landscape of your dream. It's likely that a new image forms in the mind's eye every time you move your eyes."

Nature Communications journal
11 August 2015

"Alcohol and drugs interfere with your quality of sleep but they also cut into your dream time. One or two drinks can increase slow-wave sleep while not affecting deeper REM sleep, but more than that reduces the time spent in REM."

Time magazine
8 February 2013

A study by Professor Sara Mednick at University of California, San Diego, found that REM sleep "directly enhances creative processing" by stimulating brain networks that allow for new and unusual associations between seemingly unrelated ideas.

In an average lifetime, a person spends about six years dreaming. That is more than 2,100 days spent in a different realm!

"*Dreams are the guiding words of the soul. Why should I henceforth not love my dreams and not make their riddling images into objects of my daily consideration?*"

CARL JUNG
The Red Book (2009)

TYPES
of DREAMS

At various times in your life, you will experience all categories of the following dream types, from frightening nightmares to the awareness that you are within a dream, which is lucid dreaming.

DAYDREAMS

The spontaneous imagining of events
in the past or future. You can utilize
daydreaming to reinforce positive
messages or inspire action – you get to
create your daydream, after all!

NIGHTMARES

Fear and anxiety are the common
emotions of nightmares and often relate
to waking-life situations, stress or trauma,
or reflect buried emotions.

RECURRING DREAMS

The exact same dream repeated over and over suggests an issue that you have not yet resolved. Once it has been resolved, the dreams will stop.

HEALING DREAMS

Called "prodromic" dreams by the ancient Greeks, these are warnings that can highlight health problems before you are consciously aware of them.

PROPHETIC DREAMS

These may foretell an event or situation in the future. Your mind may have pieced together information and observations to reach a conclusion that you have not consciously become aware of.

DECISION DREAMS

These dreams feature a problem or a choice before you, and they can help you find a solution or make a decision in your waking life.

PROGRESSIVE DREAMS

Dreams that continue over several nights, picking up where they left off, indicate your mind is wrestling with a waking-life problem. The different dream scenarios can help you explore various options.

FALSE AWAKENING

A dream that you've already woken up for the day. You've risen from bed, made coffee or breakfast and gone through your normal routine, only to discover it was a dream.

EPIC DREAMS

Especially vivid and compelling, these dreams evoke strong emotions. They may remain with you for years to come.

LUCID DREAMS

The dreamer has some control over the content and can manipulate the journey of the dream. Research at the University of California, Berkeley, indicates that around 50 per cent of people recall having had at least one spontaneous lucid dream in their lifetime.

DREAM
ANALYSIS

Learn ways to maximize your
dream sleep, to better recall
your dreams and to analyze the
landscape of your dreams for
deeper self-knowledge.

"We all dream; we do not understand our dreams, yet we act as if nothing strange goes on in our sleep minds, strange at least by comparison with the logical, purposeful doings of our minds when we are awake."

ERICH FROMM
The Forgotten Language (1951)

DREAMING LUCIDLY

Recognizing recurring symbols in your dreams and performing "reality checks" will help you identify that you are in a dream and, in turn, enable you to exert some control over the dream's direction.

1. Observe your hands and feet. These tend to be distorted in sleep.

2. Look at a clock or book, then look at it again. If it changes time or text, you are in a dream state.

3. Check your environment. Is it logically possible?

4. Touch an object or the palm of your opposite hand. Does your hand go through it or is it solid?

5. Pinch your nose. If you can still breathe, you are dreaming.

6. If you realize you are waking up, prolong the dream by spinning around or rubbing your hands in your dream to reduce the physical symptoms of waking up.

7. When you wake, keep your eyes closed and try to remain in the dream as long as possible. Drift in and out. You may find yourself entering the REM sleep paralysis stage again (see page 24).

INDUCING DREAM SLEEP

- Follow a regular bedtime routine and ensure you are comfortable and the room is dark.

- Place a journal and pen on your bedside table or have an app on your phone to record your dream.

- Set an intention for your dream before you go to sleep, such as something you want to revisit, resolve or achieve.

- Use a mnemonic. Repeat "I will remember my dreams" to yourself over and over as you are falling asleep.

"This is my dream and I decide where it goes from here."

ALICE
Lewis Carroll's
Alice's Adventures in Wonderland (1865)

BENEFITS of DREAM ANALYSIS

1. As your dreams are a window to your subconscious, they can reveal the desires and feelings you aren't recognizing with your waking mind.

2. Dreams help you express and confront your feelings or anxieties; thus they can promote increased self-awareness and resilience in waking life.

3. A source for inspiration, creativity and imagination, dreams can also help you discover your true goals and set them.

4. Dreams can help you problem-solve in waking life, guiding you through difficult decisions in relationships, career, home or any life issue, and relieve stress and emotional distress.

ANALYZING DREAMS

Keep a journal and write down all the detail and elements of your dream immediately upon waking and before getting out of bed.

1. Identify your emotions. Were you feeling fearful, guilty, elated?

2. Identify your thoughts. Are there any phrases that stick in your mind?

3. Where are you? Is it familiar or strange? What does the environment look like? What season or time of day is it in your dream?

4. Are you alone or with people? What is your relationship with them?

5. What is happening? What is the action and is there a storyline?

6. Take note of any signposts and symbols, such as numbers, colours, doorways, landmarks, bodies of water, animals, objects.

7. Is there any "day residue" – symbols, people or actions from the day that popped up in your dream?

8. What is the main message of your dream? What is it trying to tell you?

Finally, after recording your dreams for several days or weeks, look for patterns. Note any recurring objects, people, places, emotions or actions. What do you associate with these features?

Five minutes after the end of the dream, 50 per cent of the content is forgotten. After ten minutes, 90 per cent is lost.

Negative emotions tend to occur twice as frequently as positive feelings in dreams. Fear and anxiety are the most common, followed by anger and sorrow.

"Who looks outside,
dreams; who looks
inside, awakes."

CARL JUNG
letter to Fanny Bowditch, 1916

CHAPTER

2

LOVE and RELATIONSHIPS

Decode your dreams on love,
sex, marriage and family, and use
them to better understand your
relationships and emotions.

"Throw your dreams into space like a kite, and you do not know what it will bring back – a new life, a new friend, a new love, a new country."

ANAÏS NIN

The Diary of Anaïs Nin (1945)

FALLING in LOVE

If you are single and it is reciprocated, this could indicate that you are ready for a relationship and love is coming your way. If you are in a relationship, you may be missing an essential element in your current love life.

SECRET LOVE

You have a dormant passion — there's an activity, career or endeavour that you would love to bring out into the open. Your own feelings of self-doubt or that it is inappropriate in some way is keeping your desire hidden.

DATING

You are dating yourself – you are discovering some hidden aspects of yourself, so pay attention to the traits of the person you are dating in the dream. The date can also reveal how you believe you portray yourself to others.

"*Yesterday is but today's memory, tomorrow is today's dream.*"

KAHLIL GIBRAN
The Prophet (1923)

BLIND DATE

You are trying something new and you are not sure how it will turn out. You may be committing to something you don't know too much about, but it could be exciting and successful.

AN EX

You are reconnecting with a passion or interest that you once had. An opportunity is coming to you, but do you want to revive it or keep it in the past?

BREAK-UP

This dream is concerned with an ending and letting go of something or someone. Consider your emotions carefully in these dreams. Are you happy, indifferent or distraught over the break-up?

HUGGING

If you are doing the hugging, you are holding someone or something close to your heart. It may mean you have difficulty letting them go.

To dream that someone is hugging you suggests that you need to open up and show your true feelings.

"I think we dream so we don't have to be apart for so long. If we're in each other's dreams, we can be together all the time."

WINNIE-THE-POOH
A.A. Milne's *Winnie-the-Pooh* (1926)

KISSING

If you are kissing someone else's partner, you may wish to experience the love that you see another having. But also consider the connection with yourself, as the mouth often represents your ability to express yourself elegantly or appropriately.

LOVE TRIANGLE

If you are involved in a love triangle, there may be power and jealousy issues in your waking-life romantic relationship, or your attention and time may be divided.

UNREQUITED LOVE

Your heart is unfulfilled or a relationship is causing you to suffer. It isn't necessarily a romantic relationship – it can mean you are in a one-sided friendship or business partnership.

"You know that place between sleep and awake, that place where you still remember dreaming? That's where I'll always love you. That's where I'll be waiting."

TINKERBELL

Hook (1991) by scriptwriter James V. Hart

SECRET ADMIRER

There may be some unknown aspects of yourself that you need to discover and exhibit. Alternatively, there could be someone who is interested in you but you aren't consciously acknowledging them.

STALKER

To dream that someone is stalking you signifies that there is a problem or issue you aren't addressing. Ignoring it won't make it go away.

SEX in PUBLIC

If this is associated with negative feelings, the dream may be telling you that you feel vulnerable and exposed, or that you are too concerned with what others think.

If the feelings are positive, you may desire more exposure or attention from others.

CELEBRITY SEX

You desire or connect to some quality the specific celebrity has. It can be a positive message that you equate yourself with achievement and success.

ENGAGEMENT

You may be considering entering a long-term commitment; it may be a romantic relationship but equally it could be a big project or business endeavour.

"We are such stuff
As dreams are made on,
and our little life
Is rounded with a sleep."

PROSPERO

William Shakespeare's *The Tempest*, Act 4, Scene 1

"*Those who have compared our life to a dream were right… We sleeping wake, and waking sleep.*"

MICHEL DE MONTAIGNE
Essays Book II (1595)

WEDDING RING

The ring represents fulfilment and eternal love. If you are not married and are given or find a wedding ring, then a personal relationship has reached a new level.

If you lose your wedding ring, there could be an unresolved issue in your marriage.

WEDDING

If this is your own wedding, it symbolizes a new beginning or transition. How you feel at the wedding will reflect your underlying emotions concerning an upcoming union or partnership, whether it is romantic, business or creative.

To dream that you are marrying someone you never met can signify the union of your feminine and masculine sides and that you are marrying yourself – you are enough.

To dream that you are getting married to your ex suggests that you have accepted aspects of that relationship and learned from those past mistakes. Alternatively, a current relationship may share something in common with your previous relationship.

BRIDE

Being a bride or seeing a bride in your dream can reflect your desire for a lasting union and security and a future that is balanced and harmonious.

DIVORCE

This does not mean that a divorce is on the horizon, but that you may be giving too much to some aspect of your life and you wish to be released from it.

INFIDELITY

Although these dreams don't predict an actual event, they can signal feelings of neglect, insecurity, mistrust or guilt in your romantic relationship. If you are doing the cheating, you may have needs that are unsatisfied, are being dishonest about something or the person you are cheating with has a quality you want or you want your partner to have.

If you are being cheated on, you may fear abandonment or have doubts about the relationship.

ARRANGED MARRIAGE

This dream suggests that you are feeling forced into something or reluctantly moving into a new stage of life. Is there a situation where you feel you have no voice or choice?

CHILDREN

You may desire to retreat to a more childlike state and be taken care of, or you need to be nurtured and grow in some way. Take time to care for your inner child!

"You see things; and you say, 'Why?' But I dream things that never were; and I say, 'Why not?'"

GEORGE BERNARD SHAW
Back to Methuselah (1921)

PETS

The appearance of pets reflects the basic desire to be cared for and to receive love. It may also indicate that you are dependent on another person.

The type of animal carries specific meanings too: a cat represents independence, a dog loyalty, a horse energy, for example.

PARENTS

Family represents your attitudes, values
and emotional responses, so seeing your
parents in your dream can indicate the
need for protection, shelter and love.

the ELDERLY

Grandparents signify a search for the love, security and wisdom they represent, but pay attention to any elderly person in your dream and their message. They may provide guidance and solutions to your problems.

TWINS

Dualities, opposites and conflicts are manifest in dreams of twins, as well as feelings of confusion and split loyalties. However, dreaming of giving birth to identical twins suggests a big burst of creativity, good luck and new beginnings.

SIBLING RIVALRY

While this may indicate insecurity, doubt, lack of love or competing interests, on the positive side, the rivalry may suggest that an alternative idea is being presented, one that you might want to consider.

OLD FRIEND

The appearance of an old friend can mean
that you are missing something about
that time in your life or that friendship.
Which memories or feelings stand out the
most about them and how might that be
applied to your current reality?

ENEMY

Representing an opposing force, an enemy can signify animosity in yourself (you are your own worst enemy) or that there is some aspect of your life in conflict with your core values.

"Yet it is in our idleness,
in our dreams,
that the submerged truth
sometimes comes to
the top."

VIRGINIA WOOLF

A Room of One's Own (1929)

CHAPTER
3

BIRTH and
DEATH

Decipher the symbolism behind
such transformative, powerful
dreams as pregnancies, births,
deaths and funerals.

"*You must find your dream,
then the way becomes
easy. But there is no
dream that lasts forever,
each dream is followed by
another...*"

HERMANN HESSE
Demian: On Dreams, Thoughts and Love (1919)

DEATH

These are powerful dreams about transformation, transition and endings that can facilitate new beginnings. If you are the one dying in the dream, what changes are ahead for you?

If someone else has died in the dream, what aspect of them is it time to put to rest or are you in fear of losing?

*"Hold fast to dreams
For if dreams die,
Life is a
broken-winged bird
That cannot fly."*

LANGSTON HUGHES
"Dreams"

MURDER

If you dream of killing someone, there is something in yourself you want to put to death, disown or give up, or it could signify you are losing self-control or have repressed anger.

If someone is trying to kill you, you may have an unexpressed fear or failure to resolve.

WAR

You may be dealing with an internal conflict or feel that your life is chaotic or you are constantly having to fight your corner.

Aggression or anger may cause destruction in your life.

KIDNAPPING

If you are kidnapped, you are being kept from doing something or seeing someone important. You may feel another person is manipulating or controlling you.

If you are holding someone prisoner, you are trying to control or persuade another or deny them their power.

HIDING

If you are the one hiding, you may be concealing aspects of yourself from others or have a guilty secret. Alternatively, if someone is hiding from you, you may feel that important information is being withheld.

DROWNING

As for water (see page 116), drowning can indicate that you are finding your emotions overwhelming and suffocating. It can also simply mean that you need to breathe – slow down and have a break or rest.

GHOST

You are haunted by a problem or person from the past. It may be someone you can't forgive, or an unresolved conflict or relationship that you are having trouble moving on from.

*"Trust in dreams,
for in them is hidden
the gate to eternity."*

KHALIL GIBRAN
The Prophet (1923)

"Why does the eye see a thing more clearly in dreams than the imagination when awake?"

LEONARDO DA VINCI
The Notebooks of Leonardo Da Vinci (1478–1519)

FUNERAL

To dream of a funeral indicates that you are burying (or trying to say goodbye to) an old relationship or something significant from the past.

CEMETERY

Some aspect of yourself or situation in life has been abandoned or lost, or you may have unresolved grief, fear or feelings of abandonment. On a positive note, this can indicate a rebirth.

PREGNANCY TEST

Taking a pregnancy test symbolizes that you are on the cusp of a new phase in life, perhaps a new job or relationship, and how you respond shows how you feel about your preparedness.

Alternatively, this could be a literal interpretation regarding fears of getting pregnant.

PREGNANCY

A positive dream of creativity and growth, you may be incubating a new project or business plan. You are aware that it may take a long time to nurture this plan.

GIVING BIRTH

A creative dream about new beginnings – you are about to birth a new idea, direction in life or enterprise.

CHAPTER

4

NATURE

Reveal the meanings and
significance behind elements
of fire, water and earth, as well as
weather and cataclysmic natural
events, in your dreams.

GROWING GARDEN

If you are tending a flourishing garden, you are cultivating something meaningful in life, such as a new idea, skill or relationship. It can also mean you are growing spiritually.

"All men while they are awake are in one common world: but each of them, when he is asleep, is in a world of his own."

PLUTARCH
Moralia, circa 100 CE

"I am accustomed to sleep and in my dreams to imagine the same things that lunatics imagine when awake."

RENÉ DESCARTES

Meditations on First Philosophy (1641)

FLOODS

Dreams of deluge, a tsunami or flood indicate you are overwhelmed by emotions that are out of your control or too much to handle. Allow yourself to feel – holding emotions back will only result in a torrent that could drown you.

RAIN

Represents tears, disappointment or sorrow. A storm or heavy rain may indicate a misfortune, especially a monetary one, is about to occur.

SNOW

Because water represents emotions, snow symbolizes frozen, immobilized emotions.
Are you exhibiting a cold behaviour?
Are you suppressing some emotion that needs to be worked through before it can dissolve away?

WATER

Calm water signifies peaceful, balanced emotions; choppy water, intense emotions; clear water indicates you can clearly see your emotions; murky water means you are having difficulty understanding your feelings.

FIRE

Representing passion, anger or revenge, fire in a dream can mean that you are literally "fired up" about something but your obsession might be destructive.

To save someone or to be saved from fire means a transformative change is about to happen.

"*Dreams are more real than reality itself; they're closer to the self.*"

GAO XINGJIAN
The Other Shore (1997)

EARTHQUAKE

There's a seismic shift coming and your world is about to be shaken up. You may feel that you have no control over this event, but ultimately it could be life-changing in a very positive way.

LIGHTNING

A sudden breakthrough or inspiration has come to you; you now possess a powerful energy. An unexpected change or new love has arrived.

"So I believe in fairies, the myths, dragons. It all exists, even if it's in your mind. Who's to say that dreams and nightmares aren't as real as the here and now?"

JOHN LENNON
Geoffrey Giuliano's
The Lost London Tapes: John Lennon (2002)

CHAPTER

5

HOME and WORK

Explore your true feelings, goals and ambitions concerning your home life and career choices through your dreams.

"*The greatest achievement was at first and for a time a dream. The oak sleeps in the acorn, the bird waits in the egg, and in the highest vision of the soul a waking angel stirs. Dreams are the seedlings of realities.*"

JAMES ALLEN
As a Man Thinketh (1903)

KEYS

There is something you want to keep locked away or which only you have access to, such as special knowledge, insight or an answer to a problem.

You could soon be offered a new opportunity or be able to unlock a part of yourself that is currently concealed.

LOST KEYS

To dream of losing your keys indicates a loss of control or freedom or a missed opportunity.

MOVING HOME

This reflects a desire or need for change. Your house represents you, so pay attention to the details to understand the transition and your feelings about it.

For example, are you downsizing or buying a bigger house?

ABANDONED HOUSE

You have left behind your past and are ready to move on. If the house is in disrepair, you are leaving (or are being encouraged to leave) old beliefs and attitudes behind, as they no longer serve you.

HOME
BREAK-IN

You may be feeling powerless and that a chaotic influence has disturbed your peace. If you have been robbed, something valuable has been taken, or is under threat of being taken, from you.

INTRUDER

There is an unwelcome visitor in your home, social circle or workplace. It could be a person, belief, thought or emotion that you haven't consented to allow in, or which is distracting you from your true purpose. Your personal boundaries have been violated in some way.

UNABLE to FIND your WAY HOME

You may have lost your self-belief – you can't find your way home to your core values and identity.

"I dream my painting and then I paint my dream."

VINCENT WILLEM VAN GOGH
letter to Theo van Gogh, 1887

ᵃ NEW ROOM

Finding a new room in your home suggests you have unique talents and potential you have not yet discovered or explored.

TECHNOLOGY FAILS

This is all about communication. If you can't get through on a phone, if your emails bounce back or if there's a power cut, your communication is misfiring and you are either not being listened to or not hearing others.

The dream urges you to speak and listen more attentively.

NEW JOB

You may be anxious or fearful about new responsibilities in your life. Alternatively, an aspect of your personal life may feel like work to you.

"Don't let others hijack your dreams. Be captain of your own ship and master of your own destiny."

JOANNE MADELINE MOORE

Love & Sex Signs (1998)

SCHOOL EXAMS

You are being assessed by yourself or by others. If you do not know the answers, there is more information or education you need; if you ace the test, you are ready and confident to face any challenges ahead.

WRONG TOOLS

If you have the incorrect equipment
to perform a sport, job or activity,
your skills may be mismatched to your
career or a challenge ahead; you may
need to develop some new skills or
adapt the skills you have.

"*Dream no small dreams for they have no power to move the hearts of men.*"

JOHANN WOLFGANG VON GOETHE

"We are not only less reasonable and less decent in our dreams... we are also more intelligent, wiser and capable of better judgement when we are asleep than when we are awake."

ERICH FROMM
The Forgotten Language (1951)

PUBLIC PERFORMANCE

Whether athletic, theatrical or professional, this suggests that you have a good opportunity (and are ready) to show off your skills and talents.

SPORTS GAMES

Competitive sports concern ambition.
If you are part of a team that is winning,
you are attracting the help you need
to achieve.

If you are competing individually, your
performance will indicate how you feel
you measure up to yourself.

"When a man recollects his dream, it is like meeting the ghost of himself. Dreams often surprise us into the strangest self-knowledge... Dreaming is the truest confessional, and often the sharpest penance."

ALEXANDER SMITH
"On Dreams and Dreaming" (1867)

CHAPTER

6

HEALTH and WEALTH

Diagnose the health of your life situations and discover what you really consider valuable through these dream interpretations.

"*Dreams are illustrations... from the book your soul is writing about you.*"

MARSHA NORMAN
The Fortune Teller (1986)

NAKED

You feel exposed, vulnerable and open to criticism in your waking life. This may result from a new job or a situation where you feel put on the spot.

If you are unconcerned about being naked, you are comfortable in your own skin and happy to have others see you as you are.

EATING

Nourishment and fulfilment are the themes here. Are you enjoying the food and are you full and satisfied? Or is there not enough food? Are you afraid to eat, perhaps fearful of giving yourself what you need to be spiritually or emotionally fulfilled?

"*Dreams say what
they mean, but
they don't say it in
daytime language.*"

GAIL GODWIN
The Finishing School (1984)

TEETH FALLING OUT

A common anxiety dream, this is
especially concerned with a fear of being
unable to nourish oneself – to care for
your physical, emotional, spiritual or
financial needs.

LOSING HAIR

You may be experiencing a loss of
confidence, power or self-esteem due to
your self-image or reputation. It could
also mean a fear of ageing or death.

HOSPITAL

You are in serious need of solving a problem that affects your wellbeing and you are being urged to actively seek help from others to bring about the change you require.

BLOOD

Losing blood suggests you are worried about losing strength or vitality in some way. If you see someone bleeding, pay attention to the person – there is some aspect of them that could, in you, be draining your energy or life force.

"*People think dreams aren't real just because they aren't made of matter, of particles. Dreams are real. But they are made of viewpoints, of images, of memories and puns and lost hopes.*"

NEIL GAIMAN

The Sandman: Preludes & Nocturnes (1988–89)

an INJURY

You have hurt someone or someone has hurt you. This dream could also represent unresolved old wounds that need healing and releasing.

"Are we a dream in the mind of a deity, or is each of us a separate dreamer, evoking his own reality?"

GORE VIDAL
Julian (1964)

MISSING LIMBS

If you are missing legs or feet, you may feel you don't have the ability to take the steps you need to progress; missing arms or hands symbolize a lack of power to handle a current situation.

PARALYSIS

This is often a subliminal recognition
that you are in REM sleep (see page 24),
or symbolically you may feel that you
are stuck in a certain situation and can't
manoeuvre your way out of it, or you are
unable to make a necessary decision.

UNABLE to TALK

If you open your mouth to talk or scream
and nothing comes out, you may feel you
are not being heard, you have difficulty
expressing yourself or you are afraid that
what you say will be criticized.

"*Dreams are the touchstones of our character.*"

HENRY DAVID THOREAU

A Week on the Concord and Merrimack Rivers (1849)

TREASURE CHEST

An unexpected windfall, such as discovering a suitcase full of money or a chest of buried treasure, shows that obstacles are being removed and your efforts will be richly rewarded.

"The most skillful interpreter of dreams is he who has the faculty of absorbing resemblances."

ARISTOTLE
On Divination through Sleep

LOST VALUABLES

Something is lost to you – a friendship, a family member, a job, an idea.

You may have this dream when you are going through a change in your life or circumstances and have lost something from your old life.

AWARDS

If you are being given an award in your dream, you are looking for acknowledgement or reward for an achievement in your waking life.

If you are shortlisted but don't win, you may feel you are currently being overlooked.

"I have dreamt in my life, dreams that have stayed with me ever after, and changed my ideas; they have gone through and through me, like wine through water, and altered the colour of my mind."

EMILY BRONTË
Wuthering Heights (1847)

WINNING
the LOTTERY

A lucky dream, you have unexpectedly
been presented with valuable power,
resources or opportunity.

You may believe it is fate, but your
talents and drive have worked behind
the scenes to get you here.

"Dreams are excursions into the limbo of things, a semi-deliverance from the human prison."

HENRI-FRÉDÉRIC AMIEL

Amiel's Journal (1921)

CHAPTER
7

TRAVEL

Your journey through life is
revealed through dreams about
missing trains, flying, car crashes
and lost shoes.

"*I am told… you can only get the answer to all your questions through a dream.*"

EUGÉNE IONESCO

Fragments of a Journal (1966)

VACATION / HOLIDAY

Symbolically, this can mean you are ready to travel on a new path. What is the destination like? Does it resonate with a new career, experience or opportunity?

"*Dreaming permits
each and every one of
us to be quietly and
safely insane every
night of our lives.*"

WILLIAM DEMENT
Newsweek, 30 November 1959

TRAPPED in a PLACE

You are "stuck" in some aspect of your life. Where you are trapped indicates in which situation that might be.

If at a school, for example, it might mean that you feel restricted by your education; if at work, you might feel trapped in your job; if in hospital, you might be worried about your health holding you back.

BEING LOST

If you are the one lost, you may not know which way to turn in your waking life; you may be unsure of your direction and purpose or at a crossroads.

LOST SHOES

If both your shoes are lost, it points to
instability in some aspect of your life.
If you lost a shoe running away from
someone, watch out for danger ahead.

BEING LATE

An anxiety dream, this signifies that time
is running out in some way for you –
you feel you have missed out or you are
unprepared for an imminent event.

FOREIGN COUNTRY

You may be feeling like an outsider
in a waking-life situation, or you are in
a situation or mindset that is unusual
and unfamiliar – one in which you feel
inexperienced to deal with.

TRAIN

If you are on a train that is steady on its tracks and going in the correct destination, your life's journey is going as it should.

If your train is derailed, you may be following the wrong path; if travelling too fast, you are out of control; if you have missed your train, you may have overlooked an opportunity.

PLANE

Air travel represents lofty goals and ambitions.

A plane crash can indicate self-doubt, that you believe you are aiming too high and you can't achieve what you desire, or conversely that you are overconfident and need to take more care on the journey towards your goals.

"All our dreams
can come true.
If we have the
courage to
pursue them."

WALT DISNEY

The Goal (1992), earliest attribution

"If your dreams don't scare you, they are too small."

RICHARD BRANSON
Twitter, 19 July 2017

FLYING

A positive dream, this can indicate that you are attaining success or spiritual enlightenment and soaring to new heights.

If you feel scared when flying, you may be afraid to reach your goals or suffer from a lack of self-belief.

FALLING

A common dream about lack of control and anxiety, falling signifies that you don't feel safe or secure, or that you fear failure.

It may also mean that you are simply exhausted and you've reached your limit.

SWIMMING
or RUNNING

Are you moving towards or away from something? If towards, then you are ready to welcome new change into your life or achieve a goal; if away, then you recognize that something no longer serves you or you desire to escape it.

As swimming concerns water, these may be emotional changes or goals.

BEING CHASED

One of the most common dream plots, being chased suggests you are running from an emotion or responsibility.

If you are the one doing the chasing, you may be pursuing something just out of your grasp.

PACKING
for a TRIP

Big changes are underfoot. When you are packing in a dream, you are selecting the things you need for this transition.

Repetitious packing shows that you are feeling unprepared for the changes ahead.

"To awaken within the dream is our purpose now. When we are awake within the dream, the ego-created earth-drama comes to an end and a more benign and wondrous dream arises."

ECKHART TOLLE
A New Earth (2005)

"During our dreams we do not know we are dreaming... Only on waking do we know it was a dream. Only after the great awakening will we realize that this is the great dream."

ZHUANGZI
Kuang-ming Wu's *The Butterfly as Companion* (1990)

DRIVING a CAR

Driving reflects your ambition and ability to navigate your journey through life, so pay attention to the details.

Are you in a traffic jam? Are you driving too fast for the conditions, or is someone else in control of the car? How you feel about the drive will tell you how you feel about the path you are currently on.

LOST
or STOLEN CAR

A lost car can indicate that you feel you have lost your direction or are unsure where you want to go; a stolen car signifies that someone or something has pulled you away from your path.

CAR CRASH

This dream may be telling you to proceed cautiously – there is a physical, emotional or spiritual crash ahead and you may be in danger of making an error of judgement.

Whether you are driving or not, a crash tells you that you feel out of control and are steering towards a potential disaster.

"Dreams in the dusk, only dreams closing the day and with the day's close going back to the grey things, the dark things, the far, deep things of dreamland."

CARL SANDBURG
"Dreams in the Dusk"